Thank you Mrs. Lamie —
I have learned so much fr[om] [your]
lovely room & all your wisdom ... even one
day with you has helped my road
to a solid "K" program!

Eileen Cramer

Dear Papa

Dear Papa

children celebrate Pope John Paul II
with Letters of Love and Affection

COMPILED BY RICHARD A. KLEIN
AND VIRGINIA D. KLEIN

Imprimi Potest:
Richard Thibodeau, C.Ss.R., Provincial, Denver Province, The Redemptorists

Published by Liguori/Triumph, imprint of Liguori Publications, Liguori, Missouri
www.liguori.org
www.catholicbooksonline.com

Copyright 2003 by Richard A. Klein and Virginia D. Klein

ISBN 0-7648-1097-9

Library of Congress Catalog Control Number: 2003104315

Photographic source: 7, 23, 27, 39, 43, 47, 55, 63, 85, 93, 97, 103, 115; *L'Osservatore Romano*/Servizio Fotographico

Printed in the United States of America
08 07 06 05 04 03   4 3 2 1
First edition

Introduction

In February 2001, I awoke from a routine medical test blinded by a stroke. Suddenly, I was a documentary filmmaker without eyes. A year into my recovery, I was still feeling powerless and plenty sorry for myself, when my dear pal and part-time partner, TV producer Lou Reda, along with my best friend and full-time partner, wife Virginia, began to bug me about doing something besides watching reruns of *Matlock* and struggling through the morning newspaper. Jinny and I had worked on the Papal Visit to St. Louis in 1999—she had overseen the eighty-two hundred volunteers—and a friend and I had manufactured and marketed the commemorative jewelry.

"The Holy Father will celebrate his 25th anniversary next fall," said Virginia one morning. "Why don't we do some wonderful Jubilee project for the Pope—something with kids?"

And very soon after was born the idea for *Dear Papa*.

Virginia and I have so many people to thank. First, there is Archbishop Timothy M. Dolan (Milwaukee) who was the first to offer us his help, support, and encouragement. Then, there are the ten thousand students—aged five and up—who enthusiastically responded to our request for letters to the Holy Father. Our love and thanks also go to the legion of very devoted volunteers who poured through the thousands of messages and drawings—particularly our volunteer readers—Kass Dotterweich, Joy Dunkelman, Ann and Ellen Fusz, Mary Guyol, Joel Marks, and Janellen Sparacio. Back when the book was only an idea, a very talented St. Louis art director, Kathleen Brackeen, produced a series of wonderful page layouts for us—pro bono. Mil thanks to her. And thanks, also, to Joe and Nancy Cunningham of Creative Graphics, Allentown, Pennsylvania. They actually produced two printed prototypes of the book for our presentation to publishers and clergy. Then, there is our very special friend, Joan Lewis of the Vatican Information Service. Joan spent a wonderful week with Jinny and me in Rome—handholding us through the photo archives of the Vatican's daily newspaper, *L'Osservatore Romano*, in search of illustrations for our book. And when we had to leave Rome, she continued to search for and find the fantastic photos that fill *Dear Papa*. Our gratitude also goes to Msgr. Ted Wojcicki, president/rector of Kenrick-Glennon Seminary, Sebastian Mahfood, Coordinator of Instructional Technology, and the six seminarians who copied all of the kids' letters to disks for presentation to the Pope and the Vatican archives. Finally, we must also acknowledge the help we received from the folks at Liguori Publications. Liguori's president and publisher, Fr. Harry Grile; our editor, Judy Bauer; our designer, Wendy Barnes, Liguori's publishing consultant, Bob Byrns—all played a large role in knitting together this unique collection of photos, artwork, and loving messages which we hope you'll forever treasure as a keepsake of Pope John Paul II's 25th anniversary celebration.

Richard A. Klein
Virginia D. Klein
June 2003

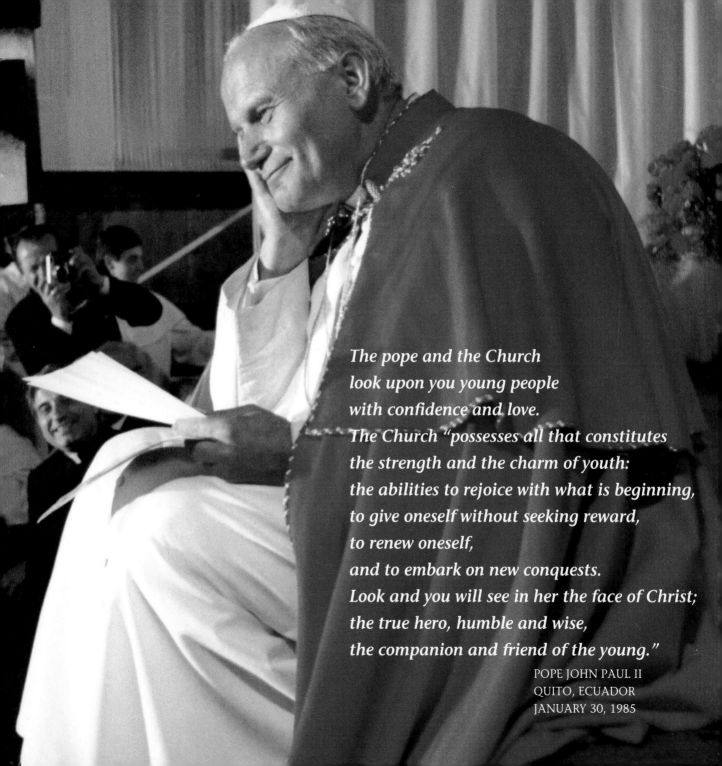

*The pope and the Church
look upon you young people
with confidence and love.
The Church "possesses all that constitutes
the strength and the charm of youth:
the abilities to rejoice with what is beginning,
to give oneself without seeking reward,
to renew oneself,
and to embark on new conquests.
Look and you will see in her the face of Christ;
the true hero, humble and wise,
the companion and friend of the young."*

POPE JOHN PAUL II
QUITO, ECUADOR
JANUARY 30, 1985

Dear
PaPa

Dear Papa,

Does being a Pope involve a lot of religion?

Zachary

Age 8

Dear Papa,

I read that you liked to ski when you were younger. I'm trying to learn, but I still fall down a lot. Is it hard for you to ski in a dress?

Sean

Age 8

Your Holiness Pope John Paul II,

Although I am not a Catholic, I still want to write to you...to tell you that the work you have done over the years, and the goodness and peace you have spread, has inspired me to be a good person at heart, as you are. I wish I could be as caring, holy, and compassionate as you are.

Very truly yours,

Jaclyn

Age 14

Artwork
by Ben,
Succasunna,
New Jersey

Dear Pope John Paul II,

I just think so far you are doing very good at being Pope. I was wondering if your Mom still makes you eat your broccoli?

Christopher

Age 9

Dear Pope John Paul,

Maybe you can come to our church. Our Monsignor needs a day off and you could work for him.

Peter

Grade 2

Dear John Paul,

My mom, Cindy, died on September 21, 2001, in a motorcycle accident. I have no brothers or sisters. I live with my uncle because he is a good role model for me. I want to ask you if you can please bless and pray for my family. We are going through a lot of changes.

Love,

Michael

Grade 6

Dear Pope John Paul II,
I hope you are happy ~~~~~~~
~~oeing pope. But what is it like being
~~, do you get a lot of freedom?
I also hope you like my card
~~ecause I went through alot of trouble
~~o make it.

Love,
Kyle

P. S. Please write back.
Gre~~
zip ~~

Happy
25d
Anniversary
Pope John Paul

Dear Pope John Paul,

    Will you tell the Lord I am very thankful for everything? The reason I asked you to tell him that is because I have a feeling he hears you better than he hears me!

               Sincerely,

               Janielle

               Age 12

Dear John Paul II,

    Do you think you will visit the Middle East soon? They could really use your spiritualness.

               Adam

Dear Papa,

    What color is God?

               Maddie

               Age 6

Artwork by Felicia

Dear Pope John Paul II,

You are a very special person to me and to the world today. I hope you are going to be the pope for as long as you wish. I'm going to pray for you as many times as I can.

Sincerly,

Chelsy

Artwork and letter from Chelsy

Dear Pope John Paul II,

You must be very devoted to God to be the pope. Most people have difficulty just going to church every Sunday! How do you do it?

Sincerely,

Joreen

Age 12

Dear Pope John Paul II,

My father and mother own an authentic Northern Italian restaurant named Arturo's. Arturo is my grandfather's name and he started the restaurant in Sora, Italy. Maybe if you come to Boca Raton, Florida, you can eat at our restaurant.

Sincerely,

Sabrina

Grade 5

**Artwork by Chelsea,
Louisville, Kentucky**

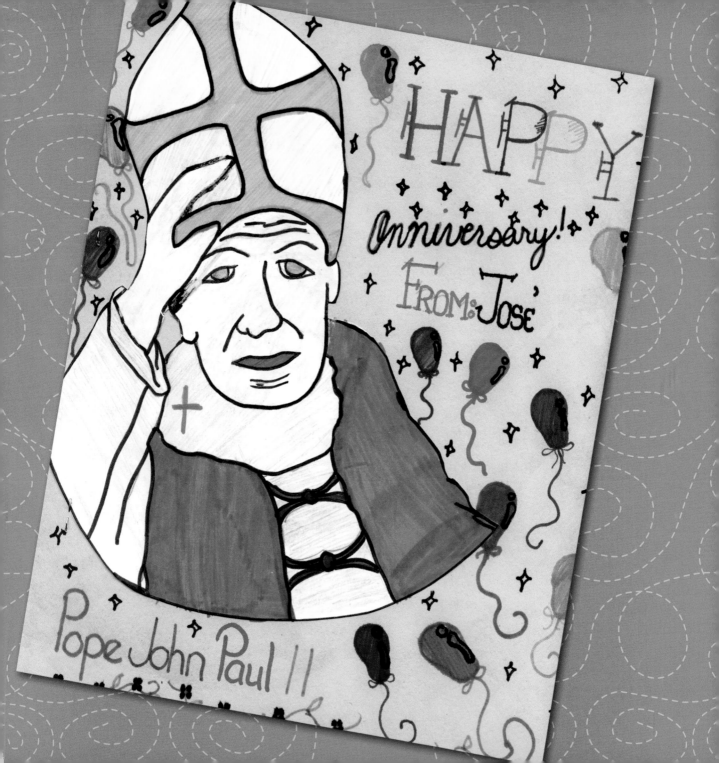

Dear Papa,

Since you are in Italy, how come the Popemobile isn't a Ferrari or a Lamborghini?

Dylan

Dear Pope John Paul,

I have a great religion teacher. I have learned a lot this year. Please write to him and ask him to pass me. Not that I wouldn't want to take his class again but I don't want to fail.

Your friend,

Billy

Age 13

Dear Pope John Paul II,

Do pets go to heaven? My cat Chester died. Does that go unnoticed?

May God bless you,

Hillary

Dear Pope John Paul II,

Where you led, we followed.

Sincerly,

Alex W.

Dear Holy Father,

What are you up to these days? School is almost over, and I am so happy. I am doing this for extra credit so pray for me. Peace out, Holy Father!

God Bless,

Megan

Age 13

Dear Pope John Paul the II,

How did you get your name? I got mine from my aunt. How many times do you pray in one day? I pray about three times a day.

Love,

Florence

Age 7

Artwork by Matthew

Happy anniversary
Papa. Can you pray
for my mom (inner ear problem)
for my two grandmothers
(Back problem and assma and
Swelling problems). Thank you
so much. Love you
Papa.

Love,
    Lisa S

Dear Holy Father Pope John Paul II,

I think everyone in the world should go to church together and then go out for a bologna sandwich after church because that's the only day my dad has off.

> Taylor
> Age 5

Dear Pope John Paul II,

What is your favorite song? Mine is "Kiss the Girl" from *The Little Mermaid.* If you write back, please print. We are just learning cursive.

> Love,
> Trevor
> Age 8

Dear Papa,

Did God ever talk to you in your sleep?

> Cassie
> Age 11

Artwork by Rocky

Dear Papa

Dear Papa,

I have a Catholic mom and a Lutheran dad, so normally, I'm trying to find the best religion for me. My dad tells me that I should follow the Holy Spirit, but so far I haven't received any signs. I am not asking for a burning bush or any other miraculous sign. Please help me.

Sincerely,

Dominic

Age 12

Your Holiness,

I hope you live to be 110 years old. If Moses can do it, so can you.

Sincerely,

Collin

Grade 5

Dear Papa,

Is your hat comfortable? It doesn't look very comfortable. I think you would look good in a baseball cap. Those are comfortable.

John

Artwork by Nicholas
Age 9
Eunice, Louisiana

25 years

Dear Holy Father,

I have a close friend who is a priest. His name is Fr. Ronald. You see, Your Holy Father, when I was born, the doctors told my Mom and Dad that I only had a one percent chance to survive. The doctors then hooked me up to a lot of machines to rest my lungs, and to keep my heart beating; my Mom and Dad called Fr. Ron and asked him to come to the hospital and baptize me, and he did. He came to visit me a few times after that and prayed by my bedside with my parents. After about three weeks, my health improved. Fr. Ron called me his miracle baby, and still does today.

I wish you good health and many more years as our Holy Father.

> A Child of God,
> Timothy
> Age 9

Illustration of Pope John Paul II by Brett

Dear Papa,

    I like going to movies with my friends. Do you still talk to your old friends that you had before you became the Pope? Or did you have to make new friends all over again?

              Love,

              Stacey

              Age 13

Dear Pope John Paul II,

    In heaven, can't Jesus make us "good" so we don't have to go to hell? Why do we even have to die? I'm sorry that I had to say hell, but I didn't know how to describe it. That word is also inside the Bible so I guess it's not that bad to say in this letter.

              Love,

              Amanda

Artwork by Megan

Portrait of Pope John Paul II by Lilly,
Prairie Village, Kansas

Dear Pope John Paul II,

I have a lot of problems in my house. My Mom and Dad are having a lot of fights. Pope, what do you think I should do? I get pretty sad when my parents start to argue. I wish they would stop fighting because I don't want them to have a divorce.

Sincerely,
Roberto
Age 12

Dear Papa,

Do you shower in holy water?

Matthew
Age 14

Artwork by Brandon

Dear Papa,
Do You like french fries?

Dear Papa,

Why did Paul write so many letters to the Corinthians? Did they ever write back?

Nancy

Age 9

Dear Pope John Paul II,

I came from Russia. My family adopted me. In Russia I prayed to God to give me a family. I prayed for 3 years and God answered me. On May 19, 2000, I was adopted. If you believe in God, anything is peaceable.

Brother in Christ,

Luke

Age 12

Dear Papa,

How do good people go bad?

Kurt

Age 6

Drawing by Mackenzie, Age 6

Happy 25th
ANNI VERSARY
God bless you
Congratulations on those
25 years.
Love,
Jordan
God bless you
Achoo—

Dear Holy Father,

My favorite saying in the Bible is "Love your enemies." That is my favorite saying because of the war. I believe that we should make friends with them because I don't like the war, and I believe that no one likes war. And plus—why kill people?

God Bless You,
Brandie
Age 12

Dear Pope John Paul the II,

Do you like your job?

Love,
Janine
Age 7

Heart illustration by Traci

Dear Papa,

How many times do you go to church a week? Do you have a church named after you? I don't have one named after me, even though I go three times a week.

Leigh
Age 11

Portrait of
Pope John Paul II
by Elizabeth

Dear Papa

Dear Pope,

I want you to help me with the following problem. I am too disorgenised and I don't listen to older people. Can you tell God to help me in these 2 problems please?

We live in Reynosa, Mexico. Every day we go by the bridge to Pharr, Texas. It is nice living where I live in Reynosa.

I love you,

Mauricio

Age 10

Dear Papa,

I made a confession on Sunday. Do I ever have to do it again?

Dennis

Age 7

Dear Papa,

Would you like being a pope more than anything else? I would want to be a pope if I didn't make it into football or any other sports.

Michael

Age 10

Artwork by Jaci

Dear Papa

Dear Papa,

I was walking, nowhere in particular, and suddenly I saw an ant colony. I was tempted and went over and stepped on it. I can imagine I killed quite a few ants and caused a few others some stress. By doing this small action, I have broken two commandments, you shall not kill and be nice to your neighbor. Would this be considered a sin? If it would be, then I have sinned quite a few times because that wasn't the first time I've done that.

God Bless,
Katy
Age 12

Artwork by Carolina

Dear PaPa

Dear Papa,

One time my Mom went hiking with my Dad to see you in Denver. My Mom said there were lots of people. I was in my Mom's stomach so I was there too.

Love,

Trevor

Age 8

Dear Holy Father,

I really admire how you take care of all your responsibilities. I can barely finish my homework.

Sincerely,

Yesenia

Age 12

Artwork by Bruce

Come to the shores of the Lord with Praise!

Happy 25th

from Sam

Dear Papa

Dear Pope John Paul II,

I live on Kodiak Island in Alaska. I will soon be moving (again) though. I have lived here for three years, but I have to leave because my dad is transferring out. My dad is in the U.S. Coast Guard. It is so hard always moving to new places and making new friends. I just became used to my school, house, and friends. Now I have to leave them behind! I feel like a dog on a leash because I'm dragged around so much.

I wish not to be mad at my dad. It isn't my dad's fault that our life changes so often. I also wish to be thankful for the things I have. You are a wonderful role model and I just hope to become as holy, forgiving, and unselfish as you.

Your admirer,
Jessica
Age 13

**Portrait of Pope John Paul II by Benjamin,
Lincoln, Nebraska**

Dear Pope,

What is your definition of holy?

Riley

Age 10

Dear Pope John Paul II,

My favorite foods are pickles, hot dogs, pizza, gum, marshmallows, and cake frosting. What are yours? Being Pope must be really hard, but you make it look easy.

Best Wishes,

Toni

Grade 5

Illustration of Pope John Paul II by Jacqueline

Pope John
Paul II
Help us!

ALLELUIA

Dear Pope John Paul II
I hoping your having a
nice day. Can you help
me influence like you?

Please help me,
Michael

At: St. Pius school

Dear Pope John Paul II,

I was wondering if you ever felt excluded among the kids at your school. The reason I ask is that recently I've been feeling like I don't fit in. I try to fit into this group, but they don't seem to want to be around me. I never used to have trouble making friends, but recently it's almost like everyone is trying to hide something from me. I don't know what to do. It makes me feel so hurt deep down. Do you have any suggestions for me? Thank you for listening.

God Bless,

Jess

Age 13

Dear Pope John Paul II,

What kind of gas does the Popemobile use? Have many long, happy, healthy years.

Ungel

Age 7

Artwork by Brian

Your Holiness,

If you were sick, do you have a substitute to come in for you? Do you go to movie theaters? What's your favorite movie? I'm sorry if these are silly questions but this is what goes on in kids' heads sometimes.

Sincerely,

Amanda

Age 8

Dear Papa,

First I'd like to tell you that I'm a Muslim. I really respect all the other students who are Christian and I believe that they are also respectful of my beliefs. Almost all the people I know that are Christian are very well mannered and kind. I think the world today is such a place because of leaders like you, and I want to thank you for that.

Love,

Shireen

Age 14

Dear Holy Father,

Congratulations! Happy 25th Anniversary Pope John Paul! You'r a great, nice, loving, and wonderful Pope. I hope I can visit you in Rome some time. If I can, I'd be so happy to visit with you.

Your daughter in Christ,
Corri A.

Dear Holy Father,

My dad recently quit his job. But you can't quit being pope, can you?

Sincerely,

Claire

Age 13

Dear Pope John Paul II,

How come prayers sometimes do not work?

Sincerely,

Jonathan

Age 10

Dear Papa,

How can they come up with all of the different religions like Catholic, Lutheran, Methodist, Presbyterian, and all the others?

Love,

Grant

Grade 2

Dear Papa,
How did you like the resurrection?
from John, age 8
P.S. Good bye

Dear Papa,

Do you know how many Popes there has been? I have memorized all 43 presidents of the U.S. and someday I want to memorize all the popes.

Thank you so much,
Mitchell
Age 9

Dear Pope John Paul,

When it was raining real hard and there were lots of puddles to jump in, did your Mom say you can't go out? That's what my Mom says, that stinks doesn't it?

Sincerely,
Steven
Age 10

Drawing of a ladybug by Mackenzie, age 6

Dear Papa,
I Love You.
I Just Wanted To Tell You That before I Fall
Asleep At Night I Say Hail Mary's. When I Have
A bad Dream I Think Of You And Then My
Dream Isn't Bad any More. I Want To Meet You.
                    Love,
                    Alexis

Dear Papa

Dear Papa,

I am not Catholic but I might become one. It's a hard decision because my mom wants me to, but I don't. I don't want to because I don't want to do confession or I might embarrass myself. Tell me if you think I should become a Catholic.

Sincerely,

John

Age 10

Dear Holy Father,

Could you make one big tent for everyone in the world to get together? We could all pray under it if you want.

Andrew

Age 5

Dear Pope John,

Were you holy when you were a child? Were you talkative when you were young? What did you do to stop your bad habits? (I need suggestions.)

Bye,

Ogeclù

Dear Papa,

I would like to know if God will send you to hell if you don't follow the commandments fully, you just mess them up a little but not actually break them? I want to know this because I know I am going to mess up a little bit in life but I still want to go to heaven.

God bless you always,

Kalanie

Age 12

Dear Papa,

I like your big necklace with the cross on it. Do you have grandmas and grandpas? Were you naughty when you were a little boy?

Maxwell

Age 5

Drawing of a butterfly by Hope

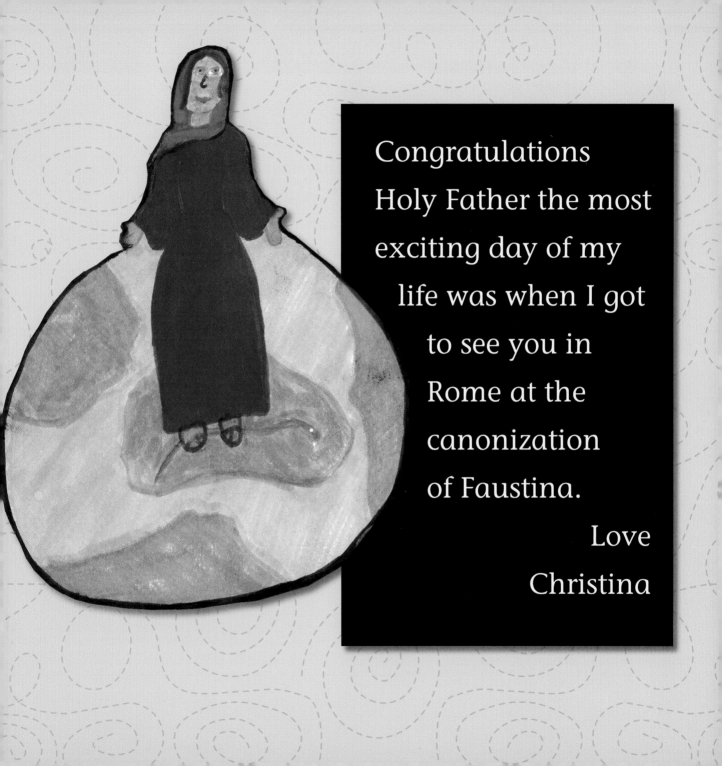

Congratulations
Holy Father the most
exciting day of my
life was when I got
to see you in
Rome at the
canonization
of Faustina.

Love
Christina

Dear Pope John Paul II,

I know everybody else is going to write to you saying "Happy 25th Anniversary" and I hope that too, but the main reason I am writing is because to tell you how much you and God and Jesus and Mary have taken my life and turned it from miserable to <u>so</u> happy that it makes me want to cry! Your teachings of Jesus Christ inspire me <u>so</u> <u>much</u>! When I was little, my family didn't go to church and we were always in fights, but now that we go to church and I go to a Catholic school, my life is <u>so</u> wonderful!

My Mom is a huge lover of Jesus Christ and I am following her and you because I have found out how awful your life is without God and how great it is with Him! I love you and I hope that you are always guided by our Lord, Jesus Christ!

I love You!

Love always,

Madison

Artwork and letter
by Madison

Jesus Rocks!

Dear Papa,

    I just made my first communion so I have learned about sins. And a lot of people still do them. When people go to heaven do they stay in heaven or can they go to hell? It is hard to be good forever.

        Raquel

        Age 8

Self-portrait by Jessica

Dear Pope John Paul II,

I am a methodist who has attended
Our Lady of Grace in Greensboro
for one year. In my neighborhood
there are people who don't even
think Catholics are Christian. However,
I have learned that what my non-
catholic friends say could never
be so wrong. The main differences
are the church services, saints,
and Mary. Teachings seem to have
the same God, same creator, and
same theams, which are the important
parts for me.

                    Sincerely,
                    Wesley

Dear Papa

Dear Papa,

I live with my parents, who are originally from India. Did you know that my father began his job the same day you were elected pope? He tells everyone he will never retire as long as you are pope.

I had no idea that you went to India in 1986 until my parents told me. While you were there you beatified Blessed Sister Alphonse. She happened to be my grandma's teacher and close friend. When my grandma was younger, Blessed Alphonse would give her handmade handkerchiefs. She would say, "When you sacrifice something, take them and wrap them up in a bundle and offer them to the Father." I find it amazing that you have beatified Blessed Alphonse and canonized many more saints throughout your lifetime.

God Bless,
Ashley
Grade 7

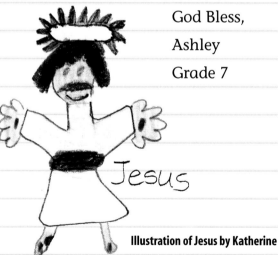

Jesus

Illustration of Jesus by Katherine

Dear Holy Father,

I was wondering if you could make the Masses shorter for little children?

David

Age 5

Dear Pope John Paul II,

Do you have Saturdays or Sundays off or do you keep working nonstop?

Sincerely,

Trevor

Dear Holy Father,

Were you ever made fun of because you wanted to become a priest and did it make your journey difficult? I am asking because sometimes I am made fun of for wanting to become a priest. Do you have any helpful tips to make my journey less difficult?

Your friend,

Josh

Age 13

Artwork by Benjamin,
Age 5

Dear Pope John Paul II,

I would like to know if it is fun being the Pope? Do you get to stay up past 9:30, I am not allowed. I have one last question, is there a Mrs. Pope?

Your Friend,

Michael

Age 9

Dear Papa,

Guess what? I love Jesus so so much my heart cracks.

Love,

Samuel

Age 7

Dear Pope John Paul II,

How are you? I have a question for you. Will I go to heaven? Do I have a special place up there for me? Can you please pray for my brother up in heaven, so that he is happy and with us?

Alyssa

Age 9 1/2

Artwork by Alyssa
Age 9 1/2

Dear Pope John Paul II,

How are you? Well, I am breathing, which is good at times! In December 2001, I was involved in a terrible accident, a rollover. One of my friends was ejected from the car and passed away. Soon after, I lost all of my faith in God. I didn't understand why it happened.

Finally, I came to the realization that it did happen for some odd reasons. It wasn't my fault; unfortunately, I was driving, and unfortunately, it was her time to go. The main thing Jenny wanted to do was to help others....In the end, she helped twelve people by being a donor.

As of now, I am rebuilding my faith, and I thank you for being a great model to guide me on my way.

Sincerely,
Jennifer
Age 17

Artwork by Regan

Artwork by Kristin

Dear Papa

Dear Papa,

    If God made us in his own image, then why didn't He make us perfect?

                Amy

                Age 10

Dear Papa,

    Why did God make Himself invisible?

                Billie Jo

                Age 11

Dear Pope,

    I almost forgot I needed to ask you two questions. Why can't we fly like angels can? Well, that was my first question, here comes my second one. Could you confess over the phone or by computer through the Internet?

                Your daughter in Christ,

                Evelia

                Age 10

Dear Pope John Paul II,

Keep Up the Great Work!!

Brittany

Age 13

Dear Pope John Paul II,

Do you ever get bored going to church every day?

Alexandra

Age 8

Dear Pope John Paul II,

I have one brother, a deaf mom, a dad and a dog named Spirit. I named him Spirit because of the white color and also because he looks like the Holy Spirit.

I have something to tell you about my life. My life is more signing than talking. A deaf person is a person. Why do people treat them so mean?

Your friend,

Amanda

Grade 4

Artwork by Andrea
Grade 3

Dear Pope John Paul II,

Does the Vatican have air conditioning?

Sincerely,

Ricky

Age 11

Dear Papa,

Can you bless my great grandma so that she has a good time in heaven?

Love,

Brooks

Dear Pope John Paul II,

What do you like more—cats or dogs? What are your wonders and wishes?

Yours truly,

Cody

Grade 5

May Peace be wiht you.

Kevin

God's hands

Dear Papa,

I am 8 years old. My name is Kevin.

Word says you're a wise pope. Since I was four I've been asking what was God looking at before He made the world. I thought it was clear, what do you think? Do you like being a pope? On May 11th I had first Communion. It was very exciting. I felt happy.

Dear Papa

His Holy Eminence

Pope John Paul II,

I go to a small Catholic school in Colorado. A man came and talked to our class last year; his daughter had been killed by Timothy McVeigh. He was going to go to watch Timothy McVeigh receive the death penalty, but this man met Timothy's family. On the morning of Timothy's death, he stayed and prayed with Timothy's family. Thank you for not believing in the death penalty.

My thoughts and prayers are with you as you continue to lead our people during such difficult times.

Sincerely,

Kelly

Grade 6

Drawing of an angel by Emily

Dear Papa,

I would like to know if some people do not believe in Jesus? Does He still love them? I have been attacked by a dog and could you tell God thank you that I am O.K.?

Sarah,

Age 9

blod

body

Memorrys of Jesus.

Dear Papa,

Have a great anniversary. Sit back, relax, and eat a lot of cake. Well, not too much. I do not want you to get sick from all of it.

All my love and best wishes,

Caitlin

Age 11

Dear Papa,

May God bless you from head to toe—wherever you go.

Maggie Renee

Age 10

Dear Loving and Faithful Pope John Paul II,

I just wanted to share my favorite biblical verse with you. I say it aloud before I go to bed every day. Here it is: "Pleasant words are like a honeycomb, sweetness to the soul, and health to the body."—Proverbs 16:24. I hope you like it!

Sincerely,

Your native American friend,

Amanda

that's you

Artwork and letter from Jentry

and
that's me

I was hurt.

you helped.

Dear Pope John Paul,

How old do you have to be to become the Pope? I'm only ten. I don't think I am old enough yet.

Sincerely,

Keli

Dear Papa,

In all your wisdom, what would you tell the children of the world is the one thing we must always remember?

Respectfully,

Paul

Age 11

Dear Holy Father,

Do you have the Bible memorized?

Joe

Age 11

Artwork by Aimee

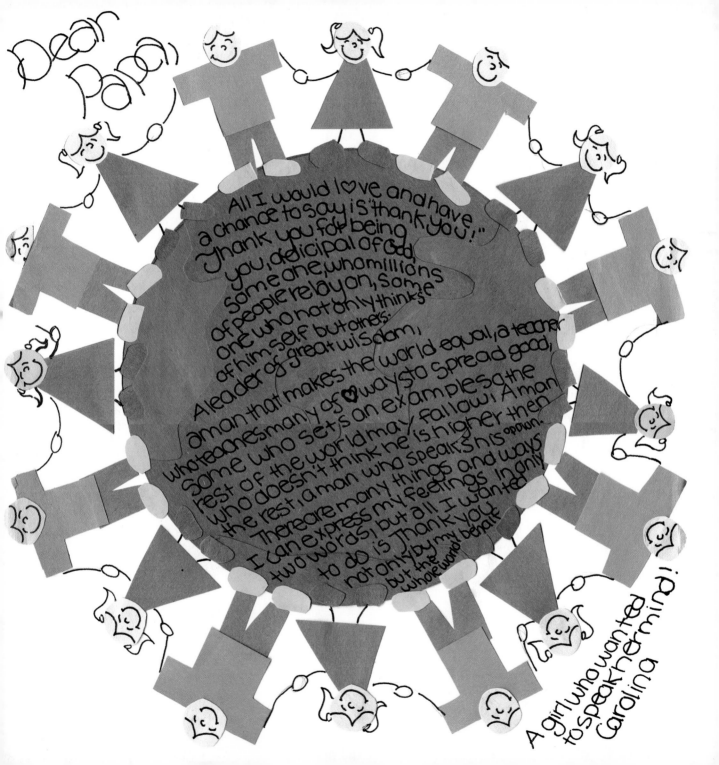

Dear Papa,

All I would love and have a chance to say is "thank you!" Thank you for being you, a dicipal of God, someone whom millions of people rely on, someone who not only thinks of himself but others. A leader of great wisdom, a man that makes the world equal, a teacher who teaches many of ♥ ways to spread good, some who sets an example so the rest of the world may fallow! A man who doesn't think he is higher then the rest, a man who speaks his opnin. There are many things and ways I can express my feelings, in only two words, but all I wanted to do is Thank you not only by my behalf but the whole world!

A girl who wanted to speak her mind!
Carolina

Dear Pope John Paul II,

I was adopted at the age of six months from Korea. I knew that I was adopted for a good reason and that God knows and understands that my birth parents were in poverty when I was born. Just not too long ago, I received an e-mail saying that I have three brothers and one sister. They are all doing fine and my parents wished me a happy life here in America.

Sincerely,

Kitie

Dear Pope John Paul II,

Do you ever just hang out with your friends like going to the movies, bowling, or bingo?

Jamie

Age 13

Lettering by Regina, Age 8
Lincoln, Nebraska

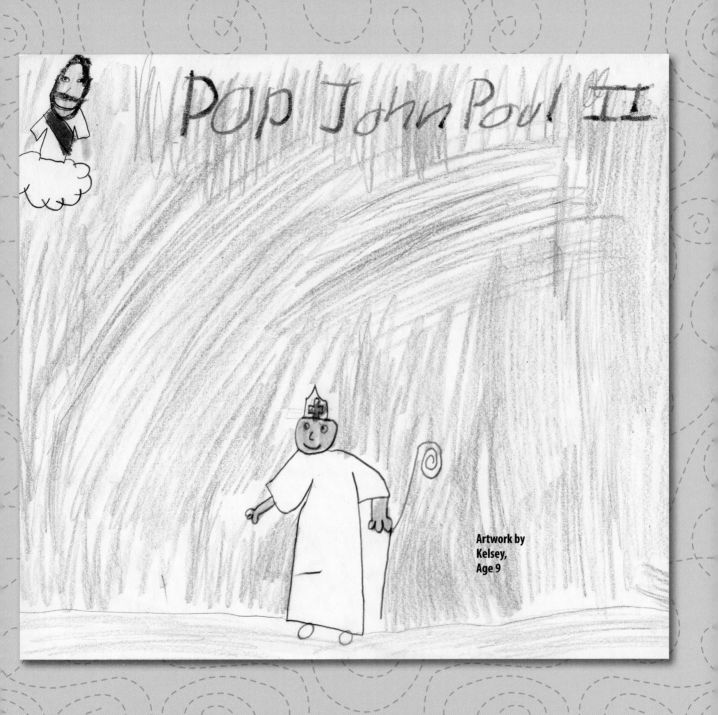

Pop John Poul II

Artwork by
Kelsey,
Age 9

Dear Papa,

Do you have to wear the crown and all those clothes all day long? Or do you get to wear normal clothes like shorts and tee-shirts? I know you probably wear sandals because Christ wore them.

Tremaine

Age 14

Dear Holy Father:

A man ran over my dog last week and killed him. All I can think about is getting my father's gun and shooting him. My mom and dad told me that a few years before I was born, someone shot you and you almost died. But right after you woke up from your surgery, you forgave the man and even visited him in prison. Am I ever going to feel okay about the guy who killed my dog who was my best friend? I keep praying I will, but it hasn't helped so far.

Fernando

Age 15

Dear Holy Father,

Will doing homework ever help you get into heaven?

Paul

Dear Papa,

If I want to be the Pope, do I have to be Catholic?

Peter

Age 8

Dear Pope John Paul II,

I speak English and Español. I am proud to be both Spanish and American. It is a great honor to open my heart to you and express my feelings. I have a strong faith in my religious beliefs and the Catholic Church, and will try very hard to keep Jesus in my heart. God bless you. *Dios lo bendiga.*

With love, *Con amor,*

Daniel

Age 8

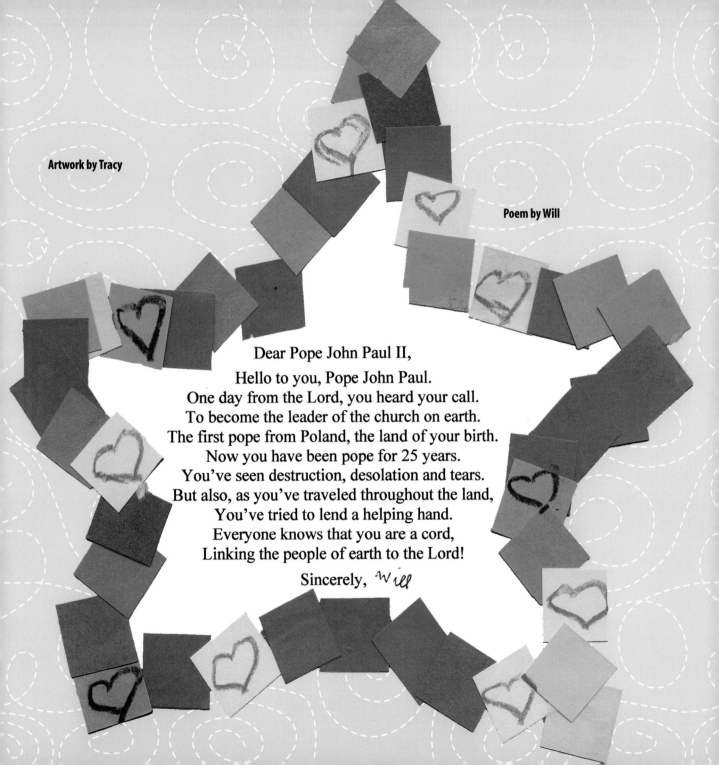

Artwork by Tracy

Poem by Will

Dear Pope John Paul II,

Hello to you, Pope John Paul.
One day from the Lord, you heard your call.
To become the leader of the church on earth.
The first pope from Poland, the land of your birth.
Now you have been pope for 25 years.
You've seen destruction, desolation and tears.
But also, as you've traveled throughout the land,
You've tried to lend a helping hand.
Everyone knows that you are a cord,
Linking the people of earth to the Lord!

Sincerely, Will

Dear Pope John Paul II,

My best friend's name is Bernadette. Do you have a best friend (on Earth)?

Danielle

Age 10

Dear Papa,

Why do we always sin even when we don't want to?

Elsie

Age 11

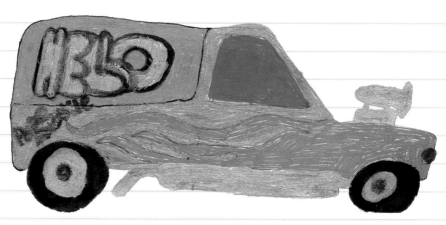

Illustration of the "Popemobile" by Gregory

Dear Pope John Paul II

Hi! My name is Gregory. What is your favorite sport? Mine are skiing and basketball and baseball. Is it cool to be Pope? My family is divorced. Every other week-end I go to my Dad's apartment. I live with my Mom. What is your favorite fruit? Mine is pineapple. Thank you for being pope. What is your favorite subject? Mine is Science. Who is your favorite author? Mine is R.L Stine.

Sincerely
Gregory

Dear Pope John Paul II,

This year I am graduating and I am a little nervous. This school has been my home for practically nine years and I do not know if I am ready to leave.

I know that by going to public school, I won't be saying my prayers out loud with my fellow students, or sharing my faith as much because I will be at a new environment with tons of different religions. Do you think I am making the right choice here?

What if I don't fit in with the other students? Will I forget about God if I go here? Without a doubt I will go to Mass on the Sabbath, but will that be enough?

With love,

Merissa

Artwork by Will, Age 8
Springfield, Missouri

Dear Papa,

I hope you have had a good 25 years as Pope, because I've seen the good job you've done. God bless you.

Sincerely

Matthew

Dear Holy Father,

Do you like snakes or alligators? Are you afraid of snakes? Some snakes are not poisonous and can be very useful. If you are in a desert, please do not touch any snakes.

Sincerely,

Jonathan

Age 7

Dear Pope John Paul II,

Do you eat alone or do you eat with other popes? When I grow up I want to be a lifeguard. I have 4 dogs named George, Spot, Ony and Goto. If you are ever in South Haven, Michigan, feel free to stop by.

Sincerely,

Shawni

Grade 4

Artwork by Jaci
Eunice, Louisiana

Dear Papa,

    I would like to ask you about some things teenagers do. For example, I have many posters of a band I really like on a wall in my room, but I also have the crucifix and a picture of the Virgin Mother at the foot of my bed. Is it still all right to have those posters? Don't worry, none of them are inappropriate. Also, do you think it's wrong for teens to listen to world music? I listen to world music, and it doesn't have a bad influence on me, but it might on others. Is it okay to have magazines on celebrities? What about horoscopes? They are in my magazines and I know they are wrong, so I don't read them, but still, is it wrong having all this stuff altogether?

                        Sincerely,

                        Alejandra

                        Age 11

Mary →

Artwork by Katherine

Anonymous

Dear Papa,

One time on my birthday my parents asked me if I could invite one dinner guest who would it be, and I said I would like to have the Pope. It would be an honor to break bread with you and God at the same meal.

Heather

Age 11

Illustration by Megan

Dear Papa,

Do you have auditions to become Pope?

Kelley

Age 9

Dear Pope John Paul II,

Sometimes you need someone with flesh and blood to look to for guidance and help. Is there anyone like that in your life?

Sincerely,

Susannah

Age 11

Dear Papa

Dear Pope John Paul II,

I hope you really enjoy being the Pope because I love being a kid.

Sincerely,

Hannah

Grade 3

Dear Papa,

Please bless everyone especially my family which has my mom, my dad, two cats, a fish, and two dogs. Oh, just to let you know, our pets aren't Catholic so bless them well. Wait! I forgot, bless me too.

Your follower,

Ricky

Age 10

Artwork by Jay

Artwork by Garret, Age 9
Westfield, Indiana

Dear Papa,

My family is tight on money right now, and I feel so bad about it. Every time I ask for something like a new book bag (when my old one is torn to pieces and I carry my books) and dad gets all mad and says things like "Do you think money grows on trees?" I want a job so I can help out and I could easily handle that but I'm only 10. I want a job in a restaurant. I'd be a good waitress.

Ivy

Age 10

Dear Papa,

Who is your boss?

Michael

Age 5

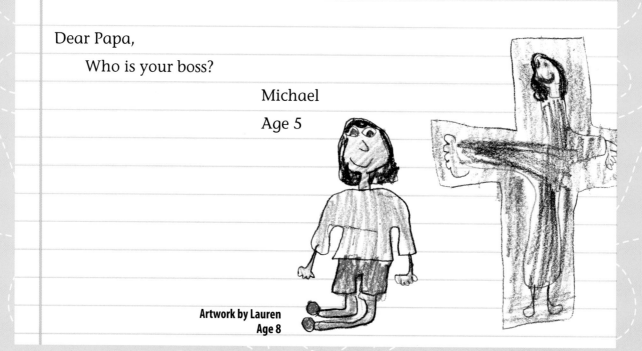

Artwork by Lauren
Age 8

Dear Papa,
    Hi. My name is Josh B.
Is it a big responsibility to be
Pope, I'm sure it is. To be one step
down from God must be a very
important job.

Sincerely,
Joshua B.

Dear Pope John Paul II,

I hope you can read English, but if you can't it's OK because no matter what language you speak, we are all children of God. I know you will get a lot of letters, but if you do see mine, I hope you like it.

Your Friend in Christ,

Rebecca

Age 13

Dear Papa,

Should we pray for the devil? I do because I think if lots of kids pray for him each day he might turn back. If he was once an angel there must be at least an ounce of good in him! Shouldn't there? All I can do is wait and hope.

Love,

Autumn

Age 10

Portrait of Pope John Paul II
by Michael
Age 8

Dear Papa

Your Holiness Pope John Paul II,

    You are Polish and so am I. Did you call your grandparents Babci and Dzia Dziu? My Babci makes great Polish food like perogies. At Easter, my Mom makes traditional Polish Babca bread. Do you get to have your favorite Polish dishes?

                    Sincerely,

                    Anthony

                    Age 10

Dear Papa,

    You know how presidents have vice-presidents? Well, do popes have vice popes?

                    Tarryn

                    Grade 5

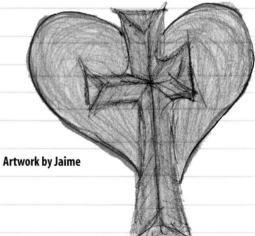

Artwork by Jaime

Artwork by Rachel
Age 9
Westfield, Indiana

Dear Pope John Paul II,

How did you feel on September 11th? I felt sad and scared. My grandmother's best friend lost her daughter, Alison, and at my school we lost three dads. I pray every day that nothing as horrible as September 11th will ever happen again.

Sincerely,

Ryan

Age 9

**Artwork by Brooke
Grade 5**

Dear Papa,

Why did God invent swear words? I mean if I'm not supposed to say swear words, why do we have them?

Your Friend,

Beth

Age 10

Dear Papa, 25th annaversity.
Happy for being a good role
Thanks and leading the church
model and leading. At this time you
successfully. At this time you
are helping the church
through a serous matter. You
are trying to make sure that
the rest of the church
doesn't fall into ruin. Thanks
for helping us out.
Sincerely,
Grant

Dear Papa,

When I grow up I'm going to be the first Black president of the United States so there would be peace in the world. But I don't make peace myself for some reason. I'm always talking back. Now my Aunt Didi is tired of me because of my mouth, and she is the most religious and peacefulest person in our family.

Sincerely yours,

DeAndre

Artwork by Joey

Dear Papa,

What was your favorite color when you were little? Mine is Pople! Ha, Ha.

Caitlyn

Dear Papa

Your Holiness Pope John Paul II,

My mother is always telling me to turn off the lights in our house. I wonder do they tell you to turn the lights off in the Vatican? I cannot imagine your electric bill.

Sincerely,

Allie

Grade 6

Dear Papa,

You must have the biggest hat collection in the world. Whenever I see your picture, you're wearing a different hat. Your skull cap must be your favorite because you wear it the most.

I have a friend who is Jewish and wears a skull cap all the time. He even wears it in school and to play sports. Is it OK for him to wear it even if he isn't the Pope? Even if he isn't Catholic?

Anthony

Age 10

Dear Papa,
Why do you carry that staff?
How many countries have
you gone to? What is the
name of that tall hat
you wear? Congratulations
on your 25th Anniversary!
Love ♡, Dani

Dear Papa

Dear Pope John Paul II,

Please pray for the terrorists to have a change of heart.

Sincerely,

Kyle

Age 9

Dear Pope John Paul the II,

Who is your favorite saint? Mine are St. Patrick and St. Bartholomew.

Yours Truly,

Samantha

Grade 8

Dear Pope John Paul II,

I hope the Lord blesses you and others. Take care of God's people for him.

Love,

Ashley Kate

Grade 3

Dear Papa,

Blake
Love Age 5

Dear Papa

me and my friends playing soccer.

Artwork by Amanda

Dear Pope John Paul II,

Do you play chess? If I could do one thing, I would play a game of chess with the Pope. I challenge you to a game. I'll be white. My move is l.Kp - Kp4.

Sincerely,

Philip

Age 14

Dear Pope,

Why do I misbehave? Can you pray for me?

Your friend,

Brittany

Age 7

Dear Papa,

If you're wondering about my faith you don't have to worry. I definitely believe in God. I thought I was going to get the flu, my worst enemy. I prayed to God that I wouldn't get the flu because I was going to go on a camping trip the next day. In about 5 minutes I felt wonderful! I was so happy I didn't get sick. God really helped me.

Sincerely,

Carlina

Age 11

Dear Papa,

What would the world be like if Adam and Eve didn't sin? Would everyone get along, and would there be no more wars? I would like that.

Sincerely,

Maria

Age 11

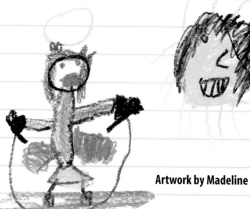

Artwork by Madeline

for you!

JeSuS   AWESOME
          God

Dear papa
thank you. I hope the picture
above makes you happy. your from
Hank

Dear Papa

Dear Pope John Paul II,

Are you allowed to wear any fun clothes when you're not doing any religious things? Also, what do you like to do during your free time? I like to read, play chess, and play with my cats. I hope you are feeling well and I will continue to pray for you.

Sincerely,

John

Age 9

Dear Pope John Paul II,

Have you ever had braces? I asked you that question because I have to get them soon. If you have had them, do they hurt?

Kay

Age 11

Dear Pope John Paul the II,

You are a great Pope. If there was ever a Christian Hall of Fame, You'd be in it.

Katie

Dear Pope John Paul II,

I want to know how to bless stuff. Is it hard to bless stuff? Do you like your job being a pope? Do you talk to Jesus? Does a pope have to be old? I have a necklace that is blessed by a pope. Many things are blessed by a pope. Have a great time being a pope.

Love,

Kylie

Age 9 1/2

Dear Pope John Paul II,

I just wanted to let you know that you are a great person, and that you are an inspiration to me. I'm trying to be more like you and one day I think it will pay off. Thank you for doing all the things you do to keep up the good job. I will say a prayer for you and always try to do my best to do good and help others.

Kevin

Dear Papa,

Why were we made? How do you help a boy that is not nice at all?

Samantha

Age 10

Artwork
by Lauren,
Age 5

Dear Papa,

I have to wear a uniform to school every day. Does it bother you to wear the same thing every day?

Scott

Age 9

Dear Papa,

I would like to start by asking if you ever get nervous in front of those huge crowds? How do you start your day? Have you ever been in a bad situation where you didn't know what to do? I have two paper routes, one little brother, and two great parents.

Nathan

Age 13

Dear Papa,

Did you ever witness a miracle? If so, what happened?

Kevin

Age 10

Dear Pope John Paul II

How is it in Rome? Is it a hard job being the pope? I want to know because I'm going to be a priest, and maybe some day I could even be pope! I could do all the things that you do.

Love,
Mark

Dear Papa,

I wish I could be the Pope, but I can't. I'm a girl. Bless you.

Natalie

Age 10

Dear Papa,

When you were elected Pope was there anyone running against you? If I had time, I'd list off hundreds of compliments.

Peter

Age 9

Dear Papa,

I am very glad you are my Pope. You are a good pope because you help us love God. Thank you for being who you are.

Kellyn

Age 8

Artwork by Regina
Age 8
Lincoln, Nebraska

Artwork and prayer from Rachel

Praying With You Makes A World Of Difference

— With Love

About the Authors

Virginia D. Klein has worked closely with Mother Teresa and the Missionaries of Charity for nearly two decades, and was a regular volunteer in India, Nepal, and Kenya. She was a longtime volunteer with the Missouri Department of Corrections, conducting a weekly ministry to inmates. She served as Chair of the Archdiocesan Development Appeal for two years and founded Catholic Leadership Development, a program to prepare young adults for leadership positions within the Church. She pioneered the Entrepreneurial Leadership Institute, a movement to save endangered Catholic schools in the city of St. Louis. For Pope John Paul II's visit to St. Louis in 1999, Virginia recruited and assigned more than eight thousand volunteers. Among her many honors, Virginia was a St. Louis Woman of Achievement in 1999, and was also awarded the Order of St. Louis King, the highest honor given a lay person in the Archdiocese of St. Louis. She is a member of the Knights and Ladies of the Equestrian Order of the Holy Sepulchre of Jerusalem.

Richard and Virginia Klein have four grown children and five grandchildren. They live in St. Louis.

Richard A. Klein is best known as a marketing "man of a thousand ideas." He is also recognized for his award-winning TV documentaries, produced primarily for ABC Video Enterprises with whom he helped pioneer the Arts and Entertainment and Lifetime cable networks. Before his debut as a moviemaker, Richard created the very popular personalized greeting card records featuring Captain Zoom, Joan Rivers, and Rod McKuen for ABC Record & Tape Sales and personalized birthday videos for children. Over the years, he has consulted for many international companies including Wendy's™ and McDonald's™ restaurants and Blockbuster™ Entertainment. Richard is also president of The Universal Archives, Inc., owner/operators of a stock footage library, serving the television and motion picture industries worldwide. He has taught at Webster University's School of Communications and has served as "Mentor in Residence" at the Olin School of Business at Washington University. He is the author of two self-help books.